40 Hidden Facts

About

Paul O'Grady

Amazing and Fun facts about Paul O'Grady

40 Hidden Facts About Paul O'Grady

Copyright © 2023 By Dave Watson

ISBN: 9798853632547

Cover illustration and content by Dave Watson

For permissions or inquiries, please contact djb20182018@gmail.com

Introduction

In the glitzy world of entertainment, there are few figures as enigmatic and multifaceted as Paul O'Grady. Beneath the flamboyant persona of Lily Savage lies a man whose life and career have been adorned with a tapestry of hidden facts and intriguing stories. From his humble beginnings in Liverpool to becoming a beloved household name, Paul O'Grady's journey is one of resilience, creativity, and unwavering compassion.

Born into a working-class family, Paul O'Grady faced early life struggles that would shape the very core of his character. Raised by a single mother after his father's untimely passing, Paul learned the value of hard work and the importance of tenacity in the face of adversity. These formative years instilled in him a deep appreciation for the essence of life, and they laid the foundation for the exceptional career that would soon unfold.

As the curtains rose on the stage of his life, Paul O'Grady found his voice through the creation of Lily Savage, an audacious and unapologetic drag persona that would catapult him to fame. Little did the world know that beneath the glitz and glamour of this dazzling character lay a performer with a rich history in comedy.

Before Lily, there was "Blanche Savage," and even before tha
Paul experimented with various comedic acts that honed h
skills and set the stage for his later success.

However, it was Lily Savage who became a phenomeno
captivating audiences with her quick wit, larger-than-li
personality, and razor-sharp tongue. The birth of Lily broug
with it a surge of popularity, leading Paul O'Grady to conquer th
heights of comedy stardom, both on the stage and the sma
screen. Yet, as we explore the captivating world of Paul O'Grad
we discover that there is much more to this multifaceted arti
than meets the eye.

Beyond the spotlight, Paul O'Grady emerges as a passiona
advocate for numerous causes, particularly those close to h
heart—LGBTQ+ rights, animal welfare, and charitab
endeavors. His activism has touched countless live
demonstrating that his compassion extends far beyond the real
of entertainment.

As we delve deeper into the hidden facts of Paul O'Grady's lif
we unveil unexpected facets of his personality, from his love f

erature and artistic pursuits to his modest and private nature, ten in contrast to the exuberance of his public image. We also hearth surprising stories, such as his encounter with royalty, his dio triumphs, and the mysterious origins of his stage name.

this book, we embark on a journey that goes beyond the glitter d glamour, unraveling the layers of Paul O'Grady's life to veal the essence of the man behind the laughter and applause. hrough extensive research and authentic insights, we seek to ine a light on the lesser-known aspects of his remarkable life— life that has touched the hearts of millions and left an indelible ark on the world of entertainment.

in us as we unveil the hidden facts you never knew about Paul 'Grady, and discover the extraordinary story of a man whose armth, talent, and resilience continue to captivate audiences orldwide.

Table of Contents

1. Early Life Struggles:

Paul O'Grady faced a challenging childhood, growing up in a working-class family in Liverpool. His father passed away when he was just a toddler, leaving his mother to raise him and his siblings alone.

2. Undercover Comedian:

Before adopting the flamboyant persona of Lily Savage, Paul O'Grady performed as a stand-up comedian under the name "Blanche Savage." This early character laid the groundwork for his later success as Lily.

3. Double Trouble:

During the early days of his career, Paul O'Grady not only performed as Lily Savage but also had a double act named "Ginger and Tonic," where he portrayed Ginger alongside his friend George Logan as Tonic.

4. Lily Savage's Inspiration:

The creation of Lily Savage was influenced by Paul O'Grady's experiences growing up in Liverpool and his observations of strong, no-nonsense women in his community. He once described Lily as a combination of his aunts and the women in his neighborhood.

5. Secretive Tattoo:

Despite his public persona, Paul O'Grady is known to have a hidden tattoo on his arm. The design and meaning of the tattoo have remained a well-guarded secret.

6. Famous Fan Encounter:

As a drag performer, Lily Savage once entertained none other than Queen Elizabeth II herself during a Royal Variety Performance in 1998. The Queen reportedly enjoyed the performance and was seen laughing throughou the act.

7. Close Call with Hollywood:

Paul O'Grady was offered a part in the hit movi "Harry Potter and the Prisoner of Azkaban. However, due to scheduling conflicts, he had t decline the role of a ghost, which eventuall went to the actor John Cleese.

8. An Unexpected Turn in Radio:

In addition to his success on television, Pau O'Grady also had a successful career on radic In 2009, he filled in as a guest host for BB

Radio 2's "The Paul O'Grady Show" while Chris Evans was on vacation.

9.   9.Animal Lover Extraordinaire:

Paul O'Grady has been a passionate advocate for animal welfare. He once saved the life of a dying puppy he found abandoned on a street during a trip to India and adopted it, naming the dog "Shane."

10. The Magic of Writing:

Besides his television and radio work, Paul O'Grady is also a talented writer. His debut novel, "The Devil Rides Out," published under his real name, received critical acclaim and showcased his versatility as an artist.

11. Love for Literature:

In addition to writing novels, Paul O'Grady is a avid reader and has an extensive collection of books. He has mentioned in interviews that he finds solace in reading and often turns to literature to relax and unwind.

12. The Mystery of "Buster Vagabond":

In the late 1990s, Paul O'Grady released limited-edition album titled "Buster Vagabond." The album featured Paul singing as his alte ego, Lily Savage, and contained a mix of cover songs and original tracks. However, the album's existence is relatively unknown to the general public, and finding a copy has become a real treasure hunt for dedicated fans.

13. Secret Philanthropy:

Paul O'Grady has been involved in numerous charitable endeavors throughout his life, but he's often quite discreet about his philanthropic activities. He prefers to focus on making a difference rather than seeking attention for his contributions.

14. Unforgettable Talk Show Moments:

While hosting "The Paul O'Grady Show," Pau
had a reputation for his quick wit and unscripte
banter. Some of the most memorable momen
on the show were the result of unexpecte
interactions with guests and audience member

15. Hidden Musical Talent:

Few people know that Paul O'Grady can pla
the piano and has a natural musical talent. H
occasionally showcases his skills during charit
events and private gatherings, surprising thos

who only know him as a comedian and television personality.

16. Artistic Expression:

Beyond his work in comedy and entertainment, Paul has a keen interest in the arts. He is known to visit art galleries and exhibitions, and he has even dabbled in painting and sketching as a form of personal expression.

17. Comedy Inspiration:

Paul O'Grady's comedic influences are diverse and include classic British comedians like Tommy Cooper, Morecambe, and Wise, as well

as international stars like Lucille Ball. Thes
influences have played a role in shaping h
unique comedic style.

18. Pet Rescuer:

Not only does Paul have a deep affection fo
dogs, but he also loves other animals and ha
rescued several abandoned or injured animal
throughout his life. His love for animals i
evident in the way he passionately advocates fo
their welfare.

19. Political Engagement:

While Paul O'Grady is generally private about his political views, he has been vocal on certain social and political issues, particularly those related to LGBTQ+ rights, social justice, and animal welfare.

20. Lifelong Learner:

Despite his fame and success, Paul O'Grady remains humble and continues to seek opportunities for personal growth. He has expressed a strong desire to keep learning and exploring new areas of interest throughout his life.

21. Friendship with Cilla Black:

Paul O'Grady shared a close friendship with th legendary British singer and televisio personality, Cilla Black. They first met in th 1990s and quickly bonded over their Liverpoc roots. Their enduring friendship was evident i the way they supported and cared for each othe until Cilla's passing in 2015.

22. Iconic Puppeteer:

In addition to his work as Lily Savage, Pau O'Grady is also a talented puppeteer. He has ler his skills to various puppetry projects, creatin and voicing characters that have brought joy to both children and adults alike.

23. The Voice of Disney:

Paul O'Grady lent his voice to the character of Wormwood the Raven in Disney's animated film "The Princess and the Frog" (2009). His distinct voice added a touch of humor and charm to the character, making it a memorable addition to the film.

24. Fashion Passion:

Despite Lily Savage's bold and extravagant fashion choices, Paul O'Grady's personal style is more understated and classic. He has an ey

for fashion and has been known to appreciat

elegant and timeless designs.

25. The Enigmatic "Paula":

During a stint in Australia, Paul O'Grady playe

a practical joke on his Australian audience. H

performed as "Paula," a supposed cousin of Lil

Savage, without revealing his true identity. Th

audience was left unaware that "Paula" wa

actually the renowned Lily Savage in disguise.

26. The Reason Behind the Name "Lily Savage":

The name "Lily Savage" was inspired by a combination of influences. "Lily" came from an Irish barmaid whom Paul O'Grady met during his early career, while "Savage" was a nod to the fierce and unapologetic nature of the character.

27. Health-Care Background:

Before delving into entertainment, Paul O'Grady worked in the health-care sector as a social worker. This experience provided him with valuable insights into people's lives and shaped his compassionate approach to understanding others.

28. Award-Winning Radio Host:

In recognition of his exceptional work in radio, Paul O'Grady received the prestigious Sony Radio Academy Award for "Music Broadcaster of the Year" in 2009. His talent for engaging listeners and curating captivating music shows earned him this esteemed accolade.

29. The Real Paul:

Despite being a charismatic and lively entertainer on screen, Paul O'Grady is known to be quite reserved and private in his personal life

He values his downtime and relishes the peace and quiet away from the public eye.

30. Enduring Popularity:

Throughout his career, Paul O'Grady has garnered a dedicated fan base that transcends generations. His relatable charm, quick wit, and authenticity have endeared him to millions of viewers, making him a beloved figure in British entertainment history.

31. Reluctant Celebrity:

Despite his success and fame, Paul O'Grady has often expressed ambivalence towards the celebrity lifestyle. He has admitted to findin

aspects of the spotlight overwhelming and ha

spoken about the importance of maintaining

balance between public and private life.

32. Connection to Battersea Dogs & Cats Home:
Paul O'Grady has a long-standing associatio

with Battersea Dogs & Cats Home, an anima

rescue organization in London. He has bee

actively involved in their efforts and has helpe

raise funds and awareness for their cause.

33. Radio Return:

In 2013, Paul O'Grady made a triumphant return to radio with his show "Sunday Night with Paul O'Grady" on BBC Radio 2. The program featured a mix of music, chat, and anecdotes, showcasing his natural talent for entertaining a wide audience.

34. Travel Adventures:

Throughout his career, Paul O'Grady has had the opportunity to travel to various parts of the world for work and leisure. His travel experiences have enriched his perspective and influenced some of his creative projects.

35. Adoration for Doris Day:

Paul O'Grady has professed his deep admiratio

for the late actress and singer Doris Day. He

talent, elegance, and philanthropic endeavor

have left a lasting impression on him, and he ha

often spoken fondly of her in interviews.

36. Behind the Scenes:

Despite being famous for his humorous on

screen persona, Paul O'Grady is known fc

being approachable and kind behind the scene

Colleagues and crew members often spea

highly of his professionalism and warm demeanor.

37. Surprising Musical Collaborations:

Paul O'Grady has collaborated with a diverse range of musicians and performers throughout his career. From iconic singers to emerging artists, he has embraced various musical styles and genres.

38. Secret to Lily's Makeup:

The intricate and flawless makeup of Lily Savage was meticulously done by Paul O'Grady himself. He would spend hours perfecting the

look before every performance, and th
transformation into Lily was a labor of love.

39. Furry Family:
Paul O'Grady has a deep affection for his pet
and has had several dogs and other animals ove
the years. His beloved pets have often been th
source of comfort and joy in his life.

40. Lasting Legacy:
Paul O'Grady's impact on the entertainmen
industry, charity work, and advocacy for anima
welfare has left a lasting legacy. He continues t
inspire and entertain audiences, proving tha

authenticity and passion are timeless qualities that resonate with people from all walks of life.

Conclusion:

Paul O'Grady's life is a testament to th
power of perseverance, talent, an
compassion. From his early struggles t
becoming an adored television personality an
advocate for causes close to his heart, he ha
navigated a remarkable journey with grace an
authenticity. His hidden facts reveal the depth o
his character and the diverse experiences that hav
shaped the man behind the iconic personas of Lil
Savage and himself. As his career continues t
evolve, Paul O'Grady remains an inspirationa
figure, reminding us of the profound impact on
person can have on the world through their talent
and kindness.

Printed in Great Britain
by Amazon

31294980R00020